Don't Lick the Dog

Making Friends with Dogs

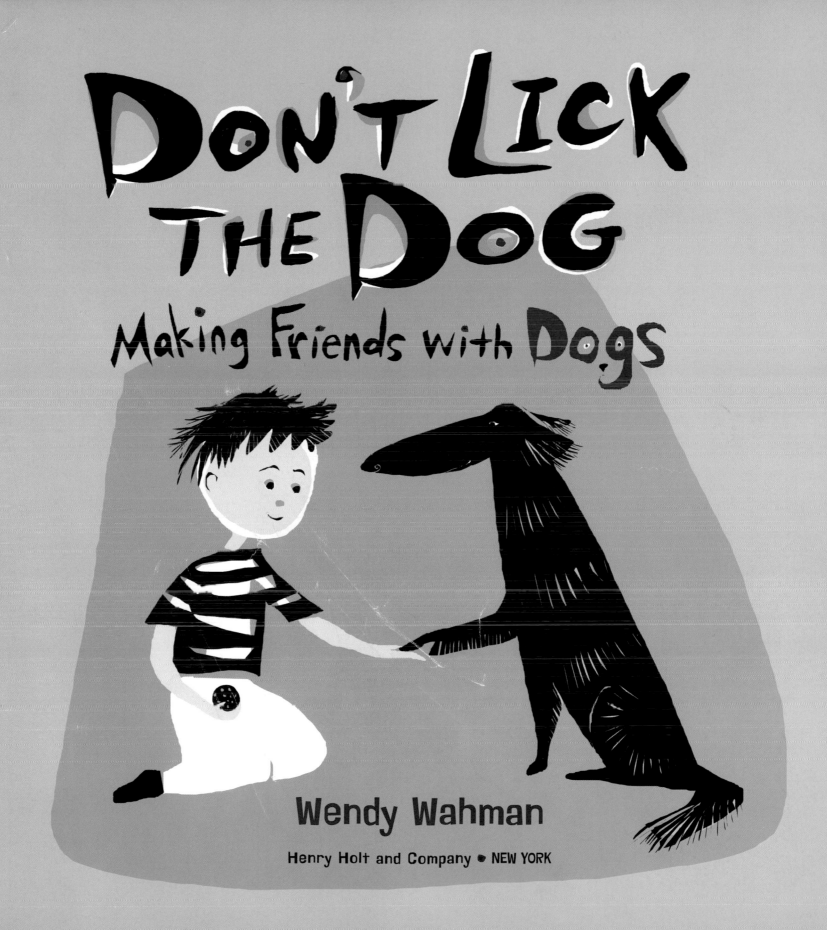

Wendy Wahman

Henry Holt and Company ▪ NEW YORK

Henry Holt and Company, LLC
Publishers since 1866
175 Fifth Avenue
New York, New York 10010
www.HenryHoltKids.com

Henry Holt® is a registered trademark of Henry Holt and Company, LLC.
Copyright © 2009 by Wendy Wahman
All rights reserved.
Distributed in Canada by H. B. Fenn and Company Ltd.

Library of Congress Cataloging-in-Publication Data
Wahman, Wendy.
Don't lick the dog : making friends with dogs / Wendy Wahman.—1st ed.
p.   cm.
ISBN-13: 978-0-8050-8733-8
ISBN-10: 0-8050-8733-8
1. Dogs—Behavior—Miscellanea—Juvenile literature. I. Title.
SF433.W33 2009   636.7—dc22   2008013375

First Edition—2009
Printed in the United States of America on acid-free paper. ∞

1 3 5 7 9 10 8 6 4 2

For Momo,
who loved children
and always wanted
one of his own

Dogs!
Dogs!
Everywhere!

May we pet your dogs?

You're so polite!
You can pet these five,
but Maddie might bite.

Easy now, take it slow
when meeting dogs
that you don't know.

Don't stick your nose in Stella's face—
until you're friends,
she needs her space.

Stand still and let dogs come to you
to smell your hand or sniff your shoe.

But curl your fingers underneath
in case one greets you
with his teeth.

Bootsy wants to run and hide
when packs of noisy kids arrive.

Turn away,
pretend you're shy.
She'll come to you;
just give her time.

Whap!
Whap!
Whap!
Dogs hate that!

Gently stroke his chin or chest
or rub his cheek—
Boo likes that best.

Before you give a treat to Kate,
make your hand into a plate.

It's all right to say

ENOUGH!

to all that
sloppy kissy stuff.

Cross your arms and turn your back
when Jake jumps up and barks like that.

Grrrrumble Rrrrumble!

Uh-oh, this spells trouble!

When Maddie makes that awful sound
and wears that ugly wrinkled frown . . .

. . . stand up straight,
stay very still.
If you let her walk away,
she will.

Grrrrrrrrrr

Dogs aren't toys to hug and squeeze
or poke or chase or tug or tease.

Just like you and just like me,
dogs have personalities.

If they could talk, these dogs would say,
"We wish all kids behaved this way!"

Good dog manners
show you care . . .

... when meeting
new dogs everywhere.